This Is How I Feel...
My Life in Verse

a collection of poetry
by
Dimonique S. Boyd

This Is How I Feel: My Life In Verse

© 2008 by Dimonique Shavon-De'Fabian Boyd. All rights reserved.
ISBN: 978-0-615-25878-2

Dimonique S. Boyd

This Is How I Feel: My Life In Verse

I dug up the book where I kept nearly every poem I've written since 7th grade recently. I sat there last night and read as many of them as I could stomach...LOL. Someone asked me awhile ago what advice I would give Dimonique the Poet at 14. At the time, I told him I wouldn't give her any advice because at every age, I wrote as well as my experience and maturity would allow at the time. I have to say, though, that it was a VERY interesting experience looking at myself through older eyes. What I did notice about my writing back then was that I used a lot of $50 words that really didn't enhance the poem, but it was my way of learning new words, I guess. I remember looking in the dictionary and writing down new words so all my poems wouldn't sound the same. Again, for 14-17, the writing wasn't bad, but looking at them now, I'm thinking, "Ick. Too RHYMY..." LOL.

I saw a lot about MYSELF at that time in the way I wrote, as well. To sum it up neatly, I wrote like other people were watching. I didn't write as much for the art of it as much as I did to release my feelings, and I find that I wrote my poems in a voice that attempted to hide my vulnerability, but in the end, there was a big TELL. So, it's like I would write a whole piece from a strong standpoint, then drop a HOPELESSLY weak and vulnerable line in there.

It also amazed me how much I "fell in love" back then. I read some really sick, sappy, poems about boys I loved from afar, and as good as my memory is, sometimes I was saying, "WHO is this about??" My pieces from high school were a trip because I was so busy trying to be, but in the end, the real me showed up anyway, so most of my work probably showed me to be confused.

I could see a real change in the writing I did when I first started college. I went from "trying to be" to defiant. At that point, I had a strong sense of who I was, and at the time, I was FIGHTING everything other people thought I was or who I should be. I wrote a lot about people trying to keep me from loving the ex, the ex trying to keep me from loving him (lol), and the movement that came about when everybody was supposed to stop perming and wear dashikis.

I guess it was toward the middle of my undergrad years when I actually

Dimonique S. Boyd

fell in true love with poetry. It stopped being a way for me to vent and became an art form. I started playing more heavily with metaphors, and went from being a person who knew a lot of words to a wordsmith.

Since graduating from Grad school, I've become a more introspective and honest writer. I write like no one is watching, or I don't care who is looking. I've always written from as real a place as I could for the time in my life I was in, but now I feel like I'm REALLY being true to myself as a person and an artist. What I really have to work on is PATIENCE. I have some great STARTS to pieces, but I'm in danger of ruining them from being in such a hurry to COMPLETE them.

I will try to arrange the poems for each chapter from earliest to most recent work, so if the first couple of poems for any chapter seem a little juvenile, they were probably written when I was a teenager, but I felt that they added something to this collection.

What I love about this book is that there's something here for everyone. You can read something from this book to someone you love, someone you used to love, someone you want to love, someone you hate, someone who thinks they know but has NO idea about you...

These are my stories. What you are reading are pieces of the past 16 years of my life. Though I take some creative license with some of the details, if nothing else,

this is how I feel...

how I feel...

I feel...

This is how I feel about...

Poetry
CHAPTER ONE
10	Lifelong Companions
11	Original Pen
13	WordLife
15	BirthWrites: A Marriage of Poetry and Hip-Hop

Crushes
CHAPTER TWO
20	Crush
21	Crush 2
22	Senses
23	Staring at the Sun
24	Bittersweet Surrender
25	Flattery
26	Wrong Side
27	Ode to the UPS Man
28	Just Friends…
30	Playing In My Hair…

My First Love
CHAPTER THREE
34	Expectations
35	More
37	Let Me Tell You…
38	Until
39	Bliss
40	Your Seed
42	Road to Z
44	Love Letters
46	Suffocation
48	The Feeling After Love
50	We: The Metaphor
53	Everything
54	I Do
55	You Make Me

57	I Love You in Hushed Tones
58	I Will Only Love You
59	Typed Tears
60	Untitled-A Poem about the Seasons
61	Goodbye
62	Getting Over…
64	Case Closed: Another damned poem about the Ex who was never my man

Perceptions
CHAPTER FOUR

68	Mirror, Mirror
69	No Less Black (Black is…)
71	UnCommissioned Portraits
72	Naked
74	UnConscious
77	WordWrath
79	Explanation/Freeing Myself
81	Beautiful

Sensuality/Sexuality
CHAPTER FIVE

84	Sin
85	Selfish
86	WordPlay
88	WordPlay 2
90	Secret
92	Pheromoans
94	Wanting...

Male/Female Relationships
CHAPTER SIX

98	I Can
101	Hard Girl
104	CockStar
107	Eve
109	I Hate Love

CHAPTER ONE

This is how I feel about Poetry

Dimonique S. Boyd

I've been a writer for MANY years, but I didn't start out as a poet, per se. In school, whenever there was a creative writing assignment, I chose poetry because it seemed like the easiest option. Sixteen measly lines that rhyme? I could do that in my sleep... What I REALLY started out being into was rap and songwriting. When I was 11, the boys in the neighborhood started writing rap songs, and I decided to join in. The next thing I knew, I was being chased down the street by a pack of boys who had been angered by my lyrics...lol. I continued writing raps through middle school.

In high school, I met my buddy Ken Whittaker on whom I soon developed a crush. He was a poet, and challenged me to just sit down and write whatever came to mind. That day, I wrote the first poem that I wasn't being graded on. It wasn't all that good, but it was mine! After that initial piece, I used poetry to deal with the growing feelings I had for him. After my feelings for him grew, exploded, and died, I used poetry to deal with my feelings about everything else.

Poetry is everything to me. It's the way I communicate in a world that doesn't hear me. It's therapy in a world that doesn't understand me. It's freedom in a world that doesn't find my outbursts acceptable. I use poetry to express my creativity as well as my emotions, thoughts, hopes, and dreams. It's the way I journal in order to make sense of my feelings and to say the things I wouldn't dare say out loud because I'm too shy or scared or unsure... I write not only for myself, but for those who feel the way I do, but don't have the words to express it or the courage to do so.

My poems are like my children. Each one expresses something different; has its own personality and quirks. I love every single one of my pieces for better or for worse because each piece is a part of me, and helped me through some time in my life. I dedicate this chapter to my poems. Mama loves ALL her babies...

Lifelong Companions

People who love their lives lose them every day,
But those who live in misery are the last to pass away.
I guess a life that isn't worth living
Is not a life worth taking,
But how do you explain that to a person
Whose loving heart is breaking?
How is it possible to live and breathe
When you're constantly emotionally slain?
How can you fill a person with dreams
Only to replace them with pain?
How can I face another day
When my body and soul are so weak?
How can I hold so much agony inside
That it hurts to even speak?
I tell my secrets to my pen
Who shares them with a page.
They discuss my love and loneliness.
They listen to my joy and my rage.
What I can say to no one else,
They always understand.
When I need someone to talk to,
I need only take pen in hand.
How would I have survived so long
If not for pad and pen?
They many not give me any advice,
But at least they always listen.

Dimonique S. Boyd

Original Pen

How many ways can I say,
"You came along at a time when I stopped believing"?
or
"You cheated, so I'm leaving"?
How many ways can I draft a four-page letter called a poem
That all boils down to,
"I love you and you hurt me"?
How many similies and metaphors can I implore
To describe my loneliness, my desires, my ire?
How many ways can I simplify Life's complexities
And confound the simplistic?
How many times can I flip my body inside-out
And let my emotions fall on the page
Before I exhaust all means of creative expression?
Somehow, I don't believe that there is an original thought left.
How many chocolate nipples and quivering pussies can I read about?
How many breathless kisses can I write about?
How many accounts of heat prickled skin
Dancing in sin
Children's grins
Can flow from the tip of my pen
Before all that can ever be said
Is said?
Well, I can't stop saying
Until I'm dead
Because I have these thoughts in my head
And they keep dancing
Keep dancing
Keep dancing a waltz through my membrane
Thoughts too beautiful to hold captive
Thoughts too heavy to carry alone
Too many pretty words for pain
Too many gritty phrases for lust
Too many ways to lament a loss of trust;
See, I need this medium.
I need to scratch my scalp

This Is How I Feel: My Life In Verse

And shake these words from my roots to my tips
From my tips to my fingers
Where they linger
Until I write or type
To give them life.
I write for freedom of self
Freedom from self
Freedom to be the self known by no one else-
I stretch my imagination in hopes of creating
An original expression
Of what are most likely unoriginal thoughts
For freedom.

Dimonique S. Boyd

Word Life

Being a poet
Is like having babies
Who won't sleep.
I give birth to children
Who won't play in the same pen
But want a drink from the same pen,
Children I can't simply
Give my breast
And rest,
Who tug at my gown
When I go to the bathroom at night
And there's no daddy to hand them off to
For a few...
The fathers never last past conception.
My offspring are a motley crew.
I've got shy ones
Who take years to be coaxed into the world
Angry ones who curse like sailors
And petal soft ones
Who just want to be loved-
I even have a few grown ones
Who are so vulgar
That I can't introduce them to people.
Being a poet
Is like perpetual pregnancy,
And no two pregnancies are quite the same...
I often carry multiples
With completely different personalities
I play R&B music for one
And the other kicks
Until I blast Creed.
Then two more wake up
No sooner than they are asleep.
My wombs has been blessed by
Rainstorms,
Heartbreaks,

Crushes,
Song lyrics,
Movie quotes,
Strangers on buses,
My confusion,
My fear,
My hopes and dreams.
And just when it seems
Another lover will never touch me,
I feel the gentle stirring
Of another hungry mouth to feed…
And I stop whatever I'm doing
To warm up my pen.

Birth Writes: A Marriage of Poetry and Hip-Hop

Dimonique S. Boyd

On the day I was born
Ink spilled
When's Mama's water broke,
And Doc was shocked to find
A microphone
At the other end of my umbilical cord.
That's why rocking it comes so easily…
It reminds me of the womb.
It's like giving birth
While being reborn.
They keep saying I've been here before,
But I've just been paying attention
And taking notes,
So take note-
I was born for this.
I'm an 80's Baby,
So it took R&B
To pacify me
I cut my teeth
On Hip-Hop beats
Was fed Funk for lunch
And had Classic Soul for dinner
Washed down with a little Pop.
I spit bars on the block
With the older boys
When I shoulda still been playing with toys
It was spit or be spat on
And my mouth stayed wet
Crushed suckas with my cipher
When I barely had my cycle yet
Many years have passed
But they won't let me forget
That I'm a lyrical vet

"This chick think she nice…"
I've been doing this far too long
Not to know how dope I am
Rhymes ain't got no track
And cats STILL hollerin'
"That's my jam!"
And I can understand
Because damn,
I just became my OWN fan.
I used to watch shows and sit back
Thinking,
"Damn, I wish I wrote that…"
Now I look back at my prose
Thinking,
"Damn, did I write that?"
Artists showing me love
And I give it right back
Cause flows can make foes
And yo,
We need to right that.
We need to uphold the code
Of days old
Before the hype of hot mics
Made bodies turn cold
When hearing Hip-Hoppers spit knowledge
Was like taking a course in college
And there was room enough
For all of us
To Be…
But if something should happen to me
Please tell the EMT
That my blood type
Is Papermate Blue.

Dimonique S. Boyd

CHAPTER TWO

This is how I feel about Crushes

Dimonique S. Boyd

I never went through that stage where I thought boys were "yucky." The first crush I can clearly recall having was on a boy in my Kindergarten class who chose me at the "The Farmer takes a wife" part of "The Farmer in the Dell." I don't think I even noticed that boy before, and I couldn't tell you his name now if my life depended on it, but something about being chosen, being noticed for a change just felt so good to me. Since that moment, I've been chasing that feeling; been waiting and waiting just to be chosen.

Sometimes a crush can be very innocent and fun. It gives you a lift having something-or someone-to look forward to when you wake up in the morning. You feel a rush when you see them and you try to look your best for them. Sometimes it's even fun agonizing over what you should say when you see the person you have a crush on.

Sometimes, though…crushes are NOT so much fun. For instance, when you have a crush on a friend, the agonizing comes in when you think about how your relationship would change if you were to take it to the next level. If you reveal your crush, it might make your friend uncomfortable and it can ruin the relationship. Maybe if you reveal the crush and your friend doesn't feel the same, THAT can ruin the relationship. Well, I have seen it all, done it all. I've been getting crushed by crushes since that day in Kindergarten.

I recently started referring to myself as "The Poetry Bandit," because I tend to serenade my crushes with poetry once I've sat on my feelings for too long. A few of the poems in this chapter have found themselves in the hands of some poor young men who were very kind, but didn't take the bait. If you've ever had a crush or been a crush, this chapter is dedicated to you.

Crush

My lips say, "Hello,"
But my eyes beg you to stay
And read my mind
So that I won't have to risk
Total mortification
And reveal myself to you.
I suffer in silence
Biding my time,
Censoring my gestures,
And weighing my words.
Which one will cross the line
And push you,
My friend,
Away?
I'm taken by the way you move.
You walk as if you have somewhere to be,
Yet you have all the time in the world to get there.
Your speech is controlled,
Yet easy and genuine.
Your eyes take me to endless possibilities
Of your tomorrow.
When I touch your hand,
I feel the smooth strokes of a pen
And the coarseness of a book's pages
Between your fingertips.
Every time I see your face,
It's like I'm meeting you for the first time
All over again.
You carry yourself in such a way
That makes me wonder
If you belong to the universe
Or if it belongs to you.
It doesn't matter.
The issues of the universe do not concern me
As long as you remain
In my world.

Dimonique S. Boyd

Crush 2

How do I begin to even say "Hello" to you?
You are the words to an Anita Baker song
And I can only sit and listen in amazement,
Wondering how something so brilliant,
So beautiful,
Was created.
Who am I to look into your eyes?
They are the portals to my dreams,
Dreams of a life with you
That I dare not imagine-
It's just too painful to snap back into reality,
The place where I pass you in the hall
Wishing I could hold your hand.
Why do I have the audacity to think of you when I'm alone?
I have no rights to your image,
To recall your smile, your laugh,
The way you look at me when you listen.
You have no idea of the way you touch me.
I know I'm not slick.
I serenade you with my pen.
I beckon you with my eyes.
I cry out for you with my heart,
Yet I cower in a corner
Afraid that you might hear me
And not want me.
I don't think myself unworthy,
But I'm probably not the image you see
When you close your eyes.
Sometimes it hurts to look at you
Because I know I may never reach your core.
I should probably know better now.
I guess that's why it's called a crush.

Senses

Someone's thinking of you,
But you don't know it.
Someone's calling you,
But you can't hear it.
Someone's kissing you,
But you can't feel it.
Someone's holding her heart out to you,
But you can't see it.
Someone's crying over you,
But you can't taste the tears.
Someone's singing you a song,
But you can't hear the words.
Someone's trying to approach you,
But you can't smell the fear.
Someone's stroking your hair,
But you can't feel her fingertips.
Someone's loving you,
But you can't see it.
Come to your senses-
Someone's loving you.

Dimonique S. Boyd

Staring at the Sun

Knowing your status keeps me quiet.
There is a "she" in my way,
So I bite my tongue.
I hold the way I feel deep inside,
For if there were no "she,"
There would still probably not be me.
I dare not daydream,
For this would be too unreal.
It is too improbable
To even be imagined.
My ever-creative mind
Can't even stretch to those boundaries,
And I remind myself
With your every smile,
With every appearance of your dimples,
With my every breath,
That this will never be.
Does it make me sad?
Not really.
How can one be disheartened
By what can't even be classified
As a fantasy?
…but I can't help but look.

Bittersweet Surrender

I gave up my wealth to touch your hand
And not a penny was wasted.
The ephemeral existence of a piece of green paper
Is incomparable to the infinite memory
Of your fingers locked in mine.
I gave up my concentration to look into your eyes,
And I've surrendered the fight for my senses.
I hardly know whether I'm coming or going,
But as strange as it sounds,
I kind of like it.
I gave up my heart to see you smile,
And I have yet to regret it.
What good is holding on to a heart
That has no reason to beat?
I gave up my ego for the sound of your voice.
My façade was broken once my name
Glided gently across your lips.
I gave up my fear for the chance to love you.
I live in trepidation of loving you too quickly, too deeply,
Only to walk away with a broken soul.
I gave up my wealth to touch your hand
But falling in love was never part of my plan.

Dimonique S. Boyd

Flattery

Can I tell you something,
Female to male?
I am sick of flattery.
I hope I don't flatter you,
Because you certainly don't flatter me.
I'm not trying to be abrasive or blunt,
Only honest.
The phrase, "I'm flattered"
Is always followed by the word, "but,"
Which,
From my experience,
Is followed by an alienating explanation of reasons why
"I don't feel 'that way' about you."
When I offer my heart,
I don't want to hear,
"Thanks, but I have one of my own,"
But,
"I'd give you mine if you didn't have it already."
All I ask is that you be real with me.
Save me the toothache-
Don't sugarcoat your feelings.
I couldn't stand it if you hurt me
By trying not to.

Wrong Side

Does it show?
Can you see what I feel
While I'm feeling it?
You don't let on,
And I guess I'm glad.
What would you think
If you knew the thoughts that spin
Constantly in my mind?
I've got to let go.
An innocent attraction
Becomes a cute crush
And graduates to a full-fledged heartache.
One-sided love affairs
Never work
And always hurt.
So why do they always happen,
And why am I usually in my regular spot
On the wrong side?
I guess the reality
Is that when one-sided affairs happen,
Both people are on the wrong side.

Dimonique S. Boyd

Ode to the UPS Man

Per our conversation...
I see you finally notice me
Noticing you.
I notice how the summer sun
Brings forth a beautiful reddish undertone
In your skin.
I notice that you always stand
With perfect posture
And that your youthful appearance
Defies the silvery strands among the ebony
Of your soft hair.
I notice that our conversations are longer
When we're alone
And how you've slowed down a bit,
Possibly to make more time for me?
But as much as I notice about you,
I wonder more.
I wonder how you manage to get a shave so close
And what you use to make your skin look so soft and dewy.
I wonder what you wear when you're out of uniform
And what kind of music you listen to in your car.
I wonder what time your shift ends
So I won't cause an accident
Looking into UPS trucks
On my way home.
I wonder what my name sounds like
Crossing your lips.
I wonder if it's enough for you
Only seeing me when you deliver a package.
I wonder if you treat all your signers
The way you treat me.
I wonder if I've said too much,
And this poem will send us back to square one
Where you stoically asked for my signature
And walked away
Barely noticing me.

Just Friends...

If you want to just be friends,
Stop sending telegrams to my sweet spot
You gonna mess around
And flood the streets
With warm, sticky goodness,
And as much game as you spit,
I'm not sure you're ready to clean up that spill.
I've got two sets of lips
Yearning for your kiss
And you ain't even true to this!
I'm not new to this
I'm fully aware
That it's probably not smart
For us to go there
But you keep me so weak
That I'm starting not to care
About the circumstances,
Consequences,
Or outcomes
Of when we both come…
To terms with what went down
When I went down…
The path that led to your bed
Or my bed
Or wherever we can give each other…
Ooh…
That's not ladylike…
But you haven't been much of a gentleman, yourself
Letting midnight musings cross your lips
Midday
And I'M supposed to be ashamed
When the thought of you crossing my lips
Crosses my mind…?
But let's back up and rewind.
We've been just friends for a long time
And I don't mind the playing and teasing

Dimonique S. Boyd

Though I could certainly go
For a little licking and pleasing…
(You did say you liked to please…)
You burn my candle
Down to the wick,
Then burn THAT to ashes…
This friendly fire
Leaves me with desires
Of being fully ignited by your flame…
But if that means
That someday
We're gonna have to figure out
How to gracefully walk away
Then I guess I can be woman enough to say…
(SIGH)
"We just friends…"

Playing In My Hair...

When I was a kid,
The boy I liked
Used to play in my hair
While he told me his girl problems,
And I would tingle to my toes
While I gave him advice
On how to win the affections of Miss Popularity,
Knowing all the while
That I would turn out the lights that night
And think about him
While I listened to my Al B. Sure! tape.
Almost 20 years later,
Cats are STILL playing in my hair
Talking bout these women
Like I'm not even there
Are you aware
That I'm a woman too,
And I might have a thing for you?
Nah…
They just keep playing in my hair,
Making it twisted and matted,
Damaging the cuticle
And splitting the ends
And I keep letting them do it
Cuz "We just friends"…
But don't friends become lovers?
SOMEtimes?
Nah…
Brothas keep
Patting me on the head
Rubbing me bald
With their good intentions…
Or lack of intentions…
Spinster Road is paved with good intentions,
And I damn sure don't intend
To spend the rest of my life being

Dimonique S. Boyd

"Just a Friend."
Some people fantasize
About being someone else…
I fantasize about someone accepting me
For who I be…
And it's easy to say
That on my worst day
I'm better than any broad you might choose,
But put up against some other chick
I always seem to lose…
Dudes keep
Telling me I'm that deal
While they playing in my hair,
I deserve something real
While they playing in my hair,
But how you think I feel
When you keep playing in my hair
And walk off into the sunset
With some other chick you met?
Someday I'll play in the sheets
With a man who'll do more than
Play in my hair…
In the meantime,
I guess I need to get a good brush
And some serious conditioner
To get these fucking tangles out…

CHAPTER THREE

This is how I feel

about

My First Love

Dimonique S. Boyd

I get kind of confused about what the phrase, "First Love" means. Can you call someone your first love even if they didn't love you back quite the same? Well, whatever it means, I met my first love when I was eighteen years old. Without going into TOO much detail, let me just say that we spent the next ten years having many ups and downs-more downs than ups, actually.
When I look at the first poem in this chapter, entitled, Expectations," I think of it as the first lie told in the relationship. I tried to convince myself that I was going into this with no expectations, but the truth of the matter was that I was hoping with all my heart that he would be the One-and I held out hope for the better part of my adult life waiting for him to see that I was the One for him as well.

As I read through these pieces with a clear heart and mind, I am amazed by how delusional I was about the relationship. As I was typing them, I thought to myself, "Who WAS I then???" I was a young woman just learning about life and growing into my feelings through my relationship with a young man.

I spent most of the relationship blaming him. I made him the bad guy who broke my heart, but I just didn't want to see that we weren't meant to be together, no matter what he told me or what I knew for myself to be true.

I don't regret my years with him a bit, because they taught me so much about myself. The best lesson I learned was that I am responsible for my heart. It's up to me to be careful about whom I let in and to be swift when it's time to put someone out.

So, here it is...the good, the bad, and the ugly. Well...you don't get so much of the ugly. I gave my journal about the really bad times to him years ago. I thought I had no use for those pieces, if you can imagine THAT... As for what's left, this is our story...

By the way, if this book finds it's way into your hands, and you know who you are, thank you for all that you've been to me, for better or for worse...

Always,
Nique.

Expectations

A kiss in the dark
A wish in the rain
Feeling his lips
Until they touch mine again
Sleeping with a fever
Waking with a smile
Feeling like forever
Is only for awhile
Holding his hand
And walking through time
Being glad that he's my man
And leaving reservations behind
Will it ever be this way?
I can't rightly say
So for now, let's be friends
Because it can't happen today.
In many years of gaining wisdom
My greatest revelation
Is that things run smoother
When you cast away expectations.

Dimonique S. Boyd

More

If you don't want to hear me,
Then close your heart.
If you have no heart,
Then I can't hear you.
If you're here for sport
Then you're wasting your time,
And, more importantly,
MINE.
I'm a woman of business
And my business is me.
A man in my life,
I don't particularly need.
I'll entertain your interest
If you respect my mission,
But if you're running a game,
I simply won't listen.
I'm a complex woman
With simple needs.
I'm sickened by passiveness,
Repulsed by greed.
Touching my body
Will not win my soul-
When my flesh is weak,
My mind takes control.
I reject your advances
Because they're premature.
I reject your observations
Because they're immature.
With hurtful words
You once abused me,
But those very choice phrases now amuse me.
I laugh at your childish attempts
To unlock my treasure-
A man knows he must touch the heart and mind
To give physical pleasure.
A woman such as I

Will not settle for lust.
She needs honor, respect, love, and trust.
So turn your back on me
If you cannot come correctly,
Because with the depth of character you show me,
Mine, you'll never be.
If you don't understand what I'm looking for,
Then simply put,
MORE.

Dimonique S. Boyd

Let Me Tell You...

Let me tell you about your eyes.
They are no ordinary vessels of vision.
To the average on-looker, they are simply brown,
But the a light hits them
And project a caramel reflection.
The African sun sets…in your eyes.
Let me tell you about your skin.
Your skin gives me a sweet tooth,
For it is the color of milk chocolate.
Your skin is soft and sensuous.
Like brown velvet…is your skin.
Let me tell you about your voice.
Low and deep,
Your voice is authoritative.
It says you are sure of yourself-
And that's just plain sexy.
And invitation to debate…
Or to bed…is your voice.
Let me tell you about your kiss.
Soft as a petal, warm as fleece.
Your kiss is intoxicating-
I lose all original thought.
It's power is two-fold,
It can either send chills
Or generate heat from my head to my toes.
An addiction…is your kiss.
Let me tell you about you.
Blackman, you honor me.
You are an example to your counterparts,
Running toward your goals at full speed.
You always dress to impress…
And you do.
You're just full of great things
And there are only better things to come.
A work in progress…you are.
So how do I feel about you?
Let me tell you…

Until

I hate the day when I can no longer smell your scent on my clothes
And I can't remember if you tilted my head to the left or the right
When you kissed me.
I detest the moment when my fingertips don't tingle
In remembrance of the touch of your hand
And my body doesn't shiver from reliving your tongue in my ear.
I rue the minute that I'm just too busy to long for you pressed against me,
Stroking my hair and whispering teasing words to me.
So your memory lives and breathes in my dreaming subconscious
And you visit my mental playground while I sleep
And you interrupt the broadcasts of my day
And I give myself to your conjured image
For you never stray too far from my thoughts.
You stay away from me just long enough
For me to miss you so badly
That I feel a part of me has been stolen
And my heart feels nearly broken,
Then suddenly I can open my arms,
Open my heart and receive you.
I open myself and swallow you whole,
Trying to hold on to you so fiercely,
So tightly
Until time steals you from me again.
I fill my heart with the scent of your hair,
The hang of your jeans,
The color of your eyes,
The warmth of the heat generated when we are locked in an embrace…
And I feel you when you are miles away,
And I see you,
I touch you,
I kiss you in my heart
Until you return,
And when you do,
I never let go…
Until.

Dimonique S. Boyd

Bliss

My eyes widen,
My muscles tense,
My temperature rises,
My mouth is dry,
My heartbeat quickens,
My body shakes.
My eyes close,
My muscles relax, but
My temperature remains high.
My mouth is moist,
My heartbeat stabilizes,
My body tingles.
My hand rests on the back of your head.
I am standing on the tips of my toes.
I am in your arms
Kissing you.
I am holding you,
Squeezing you tightly.
The moment is delicious,
And my name is Bliss.

Your Seed

You were pregnant when I met you.
Pregnant with your true existence,
And you were confused,
And you were miserable,
And you were evil…
And you spat your venom at me.
But I saw inside you,
And it was so beautiful
That I decided to be your midwife.
When you beamed,
I basked in your glow.
When your light went dim,
I tried to help you shine
And when your moods would swing,
I'd duck-but I'd stay.
And I fed your seed.
I fed your seed kisses
And poetry
And chicken and rice
And hugs
And good lovin
And letters
And full body massages
And books
And CDs
And "I love you by the atom"s
And "You're special from hair follicle to footprint."
Your seed continues to grow.
Every day, it is more beautiful than the second before.
And you shine until I almost have to look away
And when I blinked,
You planted a seed in my heart.
So we look into each other
And grow together.
Now that I am older,
I realize that the seed inside you

Dimonique S. Boyd

Has to go through a natural process
That doesn't include me.
I can watch you grow,
But only you can deliver you.
So I resign from my former position
And when you are born,
I'll cut the mid-
And be your wife.

This Is How I Feel: My Life In Verse

Road to Z

You say that you love me stronger than dap,
That from A to Z,
You feel Y for me,
But you're not in love.
You can't devote your entire self to me
Because you're trying to get your life together-
You're trying to become a man.
Well, I encourage that
Because I'm going to need a man soon.
See, I got my mind on three chocolate babies
And a long life with you.
If you proposed to me tonight,
It would be a mere formality-
My heart said "yes"
And started practicing, "I do"
Years ago.
You're showing me roads I never noticed
On this journey called, "Life."
You want for me
Things I never thought I'd want for myself
And you make me believe
That the world is mine if I claim it.
So I pray
And keep working on this Bachelor's
And map out a career path
And write these musings
Preparing myself to claim you,
Cause I'm on some Cliff and Claire type lovin.
You peel me an apple
And I'll sing you a song
After our son is tucked into bed
And dreaming of angels.
Don't you worry about being in love.
Teenage infatuation
Isn't what's going to get us
To our Golden Anniversary,

Dimonique S. Boyd

It's the foundation of real love
That we're building
As your path to manhood
Crosses my path to womanhood
And Y becomes Z.

Love Letters

If you want to know the truth,
You make my butterflies nervous.
My heart doesn't beat until you enter the room,
And even my dreams have visions of you.
I can't look at touch at the same time
Because my senses get jealous of each other.
My blush gets shy
And my silence stutters.
I feel so crazy
That it all makes perfect sense.
I've got a ten foot Jones
Running through my five foot frame
And if you don't scratch this itch
It'll be a damned shame
And it feels so good
That I can hardly complain
When you stain my lips with your kiss…
See, I write you these love letters
And put them in a pretty book
Cause I can't say this shit out loud…
Not to you.
I can't tell you
That you're included in my prayers at night.
I can't tell you
That you make everything inside me tickle.
I can't tell you
That I get so taken by these feelings
That sometimes I just cry.
I can't tell you
That I've seen our children's faces
And I know them like they're here.
I can't tell you how good your last name sounds
Next to my first.
I can't tell you that no matter what happens,
I know that you are the man I will love
For the rest of my life…

Dimonique S. Boyd

But you're reading this.
I'm scared to death
That you'll run from this love letter
I've disguised as a poem.
You say you appreciate my poetry for the art,
But you MUST know
These are more than just words.

Suffocation

I feel like I'm holding my breath
Each moment I am in your presence
That I don't say I love you.
I hold your name in my mouth
And it tastes like cinnamon
And it multiplies a thousand times
For every second I don't utter it.
Every third minute that I don't think of you,
I receive a virtual telegram
Complete with a sensation of your larger than life hand
On the nape of my neck
Accompanied by a blanket of blush
Settling itself all over me.
Now my chest is burning,
I'm gagging on your name,
And beads of blushed sweat are forming under my hair,
So forgive me for being selfish and saying that…
I love you like my lungs love air,
I love you like nudists love to be bare,
I love you like the sky loves up,
I love you like men love DD cups,
I love you like plants love light,
I love you like a beautiful woman's husband loves sight,
I love you like Tommy loves our dough,
I love you like hell, so please don't go,
I love you like stars love to shine,
I love you like seekers love to find,
I love you like a poet loves words,
I love you like a chef loves herbs,
I love you like Sally loved Harry,
And it scares me,
Because there's no off switch.
I can mute my feelings,
But you can see right through me.
I keep suffocating my heart
But you can see right through me.

Dimonique S. Boyd

So if it's not asking too much,
Please,
Let me breathe.

The Feeling After Love

I am weak for you.
For your kiss,
For your touch,
For the sound of your voice,
For the mention of your name,
I am weak.
I am filled to the brim
And overflowing,
Choking on my love for you.
My heart, Precious,
Is so full, yet so empty.
I don't know if it's going to explode
Or cave in.
I can't function.
I'm not all here
Because you have taken part of me with you.
All that is left of me is yours.
I can't fight you.
All I WANT is you.
All I want…is you.
Physically,
I can send you away,
But I can't run from you
Because you're inside
Running through my veins
Thick and warm.
You are the reason my heart beats so fiercely.
It's too late to be afraid-
I love you already.
I keep saying that I love you,
But no…
This is beyond love.
What is the letter after Z?
What is the number after infinity?
What is the day after eternity?
What is the feeling after Love?

Dimonique S. Boyd

That is what I feel for you…
   The feeling after Love.

We: The Metaphor

I stand before you, basking in your warmth.
You cast your gaze upon me.
I plunge into your eyes and I swim.
I emerge from your deep brown sea and submerge into your arms.
Our complexions mix and we become one tone.
I don't even know where you end and I begin.
I open my heart and swallow you whole.
I'm no stranger to your touch,
But each sensation is foreign.
I'm no stranger to your voice,
But your every whisper still startles me.
I'm no stranger to your lips,
But your kiss still melts me.
Taken,
Mind, heart, and body
By your every breath,
Oblivious to everything that exists outside of you.
Entangled,
We give in to our passions and begin to love.
You wash your face in my breasts while I rest in you.
I close my eyes and inhale your hair,
Becoming drunk with desire.
I wash my hands in your locks
And perfume myself with the moisture from your body.
My throat is dry.
You tilt my head and I drink of you.
You gather me close in your arms and I hold my breath,
Hoping that if I don't exhale,
Then I won't move you
And we won't change.
I could die in your arms,
I could die in your arms,
I…exhale…
And you're still here.
I was afraid to touch you lest you should run away
Shielding your heart from my rain,

Dimonique S. Boyd

But you opened your arms and bathed in my storm;
Danced in my storm with no umbrella.
You felt no need to protect yourself from me
And I wanted to dive into you completely.
There is so much danger, yet I am not afraid.
You look into my eyes, and my walls crumble.
Just come inside and take what you want.
I'll give you all that I am
And take a loan on what I am to become.
Under your touch, my brick becomes clay.
Your hands warm me and I soften.
You work me gently leaving your prints all over me.
There is no question that I am yours
And will forever be so.
I inhale you.
You exhale me.
We live on each other's every breath and I am one with you
And our hearts dance to the rhythm of each other's beat
And you take my hand
And our fingerprints fit together like pieces to a puzzle
And I hold memories of you in my heart like pieces of a dream
And people try to give me milk
When you're the cream,
And hell, I'll be the peaches
Letting you run all over and through me
Changing my fragrance and sweetening my taste
And I hungrily bite into this metaphor of us
And hold it in my mouth
Savoring its decadence,
For the thought of us is delicious
And I'm famished.
I'm starving for your touch and thirsty for your heart and hopes and
dreams and fears and tears and goals and aspirations and complications
and…you get the idea.
There's a place in you that I can't touch
And I respect it.

This Is How I Feel: My Life In Verse

You try to protect it so that others won't neglect or abuse it,
Confused about how I went from feasting on your body to hungering for your soul?
In my heart they're not so separate.
So if you're thirsting for me, I'll keep your glass full
And I'll roll the taste of you, of us, of we, the metaphor
On my tongue.

Dimonique S. Boyd

Everything

Chocolate Wonder,
How long has it been?
I'm jealous of your sheets because they get to touch your skin,
And speaking of your skin, it gets to be all over you.
I want to be everything from your shampoo to your gym shoes.
I wish I were a song so I could get inside your head
When your body gets tired, I wish I were a bed
If you're lying on the beach, I want to be the sand
If you have an itch, I want to be your hand
If you catch a chill, I want to be a sweater
The things this woman could do if only you would let her
If you're writing a paper, I want to be the thesis
If you're praying for love, then you can call me Jesus
If your skin is dry, I want to be the lotion
If you take a swim, I want to be the ocean
If you lose your cool, I want to be the ice
If you run into trouble, I want to be the advice
If you have an ailment, I want to be the cure
If you have any doubts, leave it to me to be sure
If you're sucking hard candy, I want to be the taste
If you go on vacation, I want to be the place
If you smoke a blunt, I want to be the high
If you feel joy, I want to be the reason why
If your heart beats, I want to be the pound
When you laugh, I want to be the sound
When you smile, I want to be the crease of your lips
When you take a drink, I want to be the sips
If you cut your finger, I want to be the pain
If you're caught in stormy weather, I want to be the rain
I want to be the tingle when you start to rise
I want to be the hunger in your caramel eyes
I want to be your everything, I confess
But I'll be all that you let me,
No more, no less.

I Do

I do…
Believe I could make it through this life without you,
But I don't want to.
I do…
Fear that one day this bond may break,
But that's a chance I'm willing to take.
I do…
Have the ability to stand on my own two,
But I want you there for me to run to.
I do…
Feel this world isn't fit to breed in,
But I'd willingly be the Earth you plant your seed in.
I do…
Get scared that your mama won't like me,
But I'll stand strong
If you'll stand by me.
I do…
Wholeheartedly make this commitment to you
Even after all I've been through.
I can
I will
Take all that you bring
With this ring
I surrender…
I promise
I love you
I do.

Dimonique S. Boyd

You Make Me

You make me…
Search my heart for something better to give you
You make me…
Wanna stop breathing
And start freshly to live you
You make me…
Wanna give you someone stable to come home to
You make me…
Say, "Fuck the World"
And back you whatever you go through
You make me…
See the world through honey-coated eyes
You make me…
Be who I am and drop the disguise
You make me…
Tingle to the core when I feel you rise
You make me…
Feel like a winner, cause Baby, you're a prize.
You make me…
Have coffee and orange juice dreams
You make me…
Have people question what makes me beam
You make me…
Smile so brightly my friends are blinded by the gleam
You make me…
Pray that this love I feel is all that it seems.
Although I'm whole,
You make me complete and then some,
You make me…
Question where these too tender feelings came from
You make me…
Clutch my chest to keep my heart intact
You make me…
Love what I feel and want to give it back
You make my…
Heart and soul sing in harmony

You make my…
Body sing a symphony
You make this…
The only place I wanna be
You make me…
Positive that this was meant to be
You make me…
Name children I've yet to conceive
You make my…
Cynical heart want to believe.
You make me…
You make me.
Now let me make you.

Dimonique S. Boyd

I Love You in Hushed Tones

I love you in hushed tones,
Breathy moans and deep guttural groans
Rising to the top of humid, earthy air.
I love you in short licks
And long laps
Salty and sweet,
Smooth and textured.
I love you in quick glances
And lost stares
Lowered inhibitions
And raised hairs
Unbearable flashes of heat on top of my chills.
I love you in melodies too heartbreaking to play
In words unwritten,
Unspoken,
Unknown.
I love you in places my hands can't touch
And my words can't explain;
Places where I can only look into your eyes
And will you with all my heart
To understand.

I Will Only Love You

I will only love you
So long as breath sustains me.
I will only love you
Until I can pick at the clouds
And allow them to melt on my tongue.
I will only love you
Until the oceans all dry up
Leaving only pillars of salt.
I will only love you
Until my DNA reconfigures
And I am no longer me,
And I will THEN love you
As someone else.
I will only love you
Until Forevuary meets oblivion
And Autumn breezes burn holes in the Earth.
I will only love you
Until Love itself recuses itself for all eternity.
I will only love you
Until all these things come to pass
And not a moment longer.

Dimonique S. Boyd

Typed Tears

Oui, c'est clair,
I understand you perfectly
Just because you don't want me
It doesn't mean you don't care for me
And just because you don't call
It doesn't mean you don't think of me
And just because I've fallen
It doesn't mean we were meant to be.
Oui, c'est clair
Your ideas are well-defined
Just because you touch me
It doesn't mean you're all mine
And just because we swerve
It doesn't mean I deserve you
And me loving you
Doesn't give me the right to unnerve you.
Oui, c'est clair
Yes, it's all clear to me
Years ain't nothing but time
And they won't bring you near to me
And the years aren't reason enough
For you to be here for me
And with all the tears I cried
I bet you've never shed one for me.

This Is How I Feel: My Life In Verse

Untitled - A Poem about the Seasons

It's Spring again…
The time when our love is usually at its peak,
Just before it begins its crescendo
Into the abandonment that comes
With Summer-
But we said our goodbyes
LAST Winter,
So why does my heart still remember
With such fervor
The lush lust
With which we ushered in the warm air?
We won't reconnect this Fall
But my body doesn't care.
It still feels the seasons changing
I still feel the seasons changing
And though I know
We both have changed,
My mouth still waters for you in the Spring,
I'll burn for you all Summer,
I'll be waiting for you this Autumn,
And I'll mourn you this Winter.

Dimonique S. Boyd

Goodbye

I remember a time when you told me,
"You know me, you just won't SEE me."
My heart was wide open,
Eyes wide shut.
Dismissed all the things I should have known
And made up the rest on my own.
Created a character for you to grow into,
Hoping you would someday fit the mold-
Bold ignorance, I admit.
So here I sit
Rose colored glasses removed and discarded
And I think of you.
I think of that day you told me,
"You know me, you just won't SEE me."
Well,
I see you.
And now that I see you,
I never want to see you again.
I don't wish you ill
I don't wish you well
I only wish you so far from my thoughts
That I won't recognize you if we pass on the street.
Today I claim Goodbye
And if I should never find true Love
At least I can say
It wasn't because I was waiting for you.

Getting Over...

From explicit to dismissive...
At the risk of sounding like a victim
Dare I call you exploitative?
Hell, if you exploited me,
I was your accomplice.
Offered myself up like a sacrificial lamb
Begging for your blessing
When you were no more divine
Than I.
Every breath that left my lungs in your presence
Was my choice of death
And I didn't embrace it-
I made love to it.
I welcomed death into my temple
And still you live between my temples
Riding my brain waves like the Giant Slide
(I'll race you to the swings...)
My mood swings so subtly
So swiftly
I feel so iffy
Not sure if I love you too much
To refuse you
Or if I'm angry enough
Not to take you back.
(damn...would I ever take you back?)
Really, I just want that Spotless Mind surgery
Cause I'm so tired of your memory hurting me
I mean, for heaven's sake,
This shit is supposed to be over
But I can't seem to get over
Thought for sure that this was over
But I can't seem to get over
(why the fuck is this not over?)
I evicted your person
But your spirit lays with me at night
And interrupts my prayers

Dimonique S. Boyd

And follows me to the bathroom
And it calls my name
And I call yours right back
And I'm so tired of carrying you around...
(you're so fucking heavy inside me...)
I want you beside me
But I don't think I can face you
So I just imagine you behind me
Holding me
When I just want to let you go
(have you managed to forget me yet?)

This Is How I Feel: My Life In Verse

Case Closed: Another damned poem about the Ex who was never my man

Proceedings were short, yet arduous.
We sat at opposite sides,
Ten years spread across my dining room table
No fight left in either of us
Just your truth and my truth
Finally.
You wanted to govern our adult relationship
By rules we made as children.
I pretended to believe
That you would someday value me
More than those rules…
No one was more surprised than I
When I banished you from my life
But separation proved easier in theory
Than in practice.
Though I've managed to maintain the integrity of the decree,
It still haunts me that
I gave up custody of your body in the split-
I declared myself unfit
To share you with the new chick
And though I long ago
Took bullshit out of my diet,
Damn if I don't still crave visitation…
My mind often drifts
To the scene where we shared our last kiss…
So hesitant,
Tense,
Obligatory.
Had I known that time would be the last,
I'd have said goodbye to you properly.
I'd have kissed your eyelids,
Nuzzled every lash,
Stroked your brows…
Tongued your mouth from corner to corner,

Dimonique S. Boyd

Tickled your soft palette,
Touched all your tastebuds.
I'd have memorized your fingerprints crease by crease,
Left traces of my love in between the ridges
Built bridges in the gaps between our bodies
To make them fit,
Split flow into your lobes,
Told secrets that burned in my soul
Since the moment I broke the contract
And fell in love with you.
I'd have paid homage to your every pore,
Poured all my energy
Into singing you one last lullaby
Before we said goodbye…
But goodbye is long gone
And there was more worse than better
So it's best that we aren't together,
And whether it is sooner or later
That I love again,
Our trials will now only live in my files…
Case closed.

CHAPTER FOUR

This is how I feel about Perceptions

Dimonique S. Boyd

Creating identity is hard enough without having to factor in other people's perceptions. It's natural for us to try to place people into groups-it makes us more comfortable to put people into boxes. The problem is that many times, we have no more to go on that what we see, and looks can be deceiving.

If we count too much on what other people think of us, we can become confused about exactly who we are. I can probably count on one hand the number of times per month I look in the mirror and see myself simply for who I am and not the expectations and assumptions that people place upon me in life.

These pieces are about the way people have perceived me in life-or maybe these are just my perceptions of what they have perceived...

Mirror, Mirror

The woman I see in the mirror is
Bold, beautiful,
Outstanding,
Joyous, Confident,
Proud, strong,
Intelligent, wise…
And afraid to acknowledge
The little girl inside her who is
Scared, lonely,
Vulnerable, trusting,
Loyal, honest,
Giving and kind.
The person I see in the mirror
Is all of these things.
She has been hurt
And has hurt others.
She has given love
As well as received it.
She honors and cherishes
Life, life, and laughter.
Sure, she has made mistakes,
But it's all right,
Because above all,
She is human.

Dimonique S. Boyd

No Less Black (Black is...)

In elementary school,
Good grades robbed me of my culture.
In middle school,
I was an oreo because I didn't say "ain't."
Now that I'm in college,
I have to denounce part of my Blackness
Because of the way I wear my hair.
Now that Black is the thing to be,
I have to deal with brothas and sistas who say,
"Be Black-my way."
If I wear pants,
I am no less woman,
And if I wear a weave,
I am no less Black.
I'd be beautiful bald,
A delight in dreds,
And I've been boovolous in braids.
Whether I twist,
Wet-set,
Or add a piece to my hair,
My Blackness is my calling card-
It's not something I can put on and take off.
Blackness is not FUBU.
It may be for us
And by us,
By all of us can't afford it…
Black is not what I put on my plate.
I don't have mad cravings for greens,
And I don't even LIKE chitlins.
Black is not the words I say.
It's not saying, "ain't,"
"Nigga,"
And "Fin to."
Black is not a choice you make.
You can, however, opt to embrace it
Or let it disgrace you.

Black is not my neighborhood.
I can pump my fist in the suburbs
And extend my hand to the ghetto
And help them over the wall
Or make it better where they are.
Black is not permanently setting my radio dial at the urban station.
Sometimes Alanis Morrissette feels my pain.
Since people are so hell-bent on defining what Black is,
Let's define it.
Black is "The Struggle"-
But didn't the Jews struggle?
Black is Jazz, R&B, and Hip-Hop…
But what's to be said of Cypress Hill, Jon B, and AWB?
I know!
Black is the Motherland,
Dreds, braids, and baldness.
Listen,
Just because I straighten my tresses,
I am not denouncing my roots.
I know the road my ancestors treaded to pave the way for me.
They made those sacrifices so that I could make choices.
Blackness is defined by each individual-
One shade of brown at a time.
Sisters and brothers,
Do not step on me because of the way I express myself,
Because of my words,
My dress,
My hair,
My home,
My opinion,
My goals,
My life-
I am no less Black.

Dimonique S. Boyd

UnCommissioned Portraits

People paint ugly pictures of me
Then offer them to me as gifts
And my first impulse is to accept them
Angrily and hurtfully.
But then I study every stroke
For precision
Comparing
From mirror
To portrait
Every mole
Every blemish
Every imperfection
Making sure there is no truth
In the artist's perception.
People paint ugly pictures of me
And though I can account for a few ugly marks
I look from mirror to portrait
From portrait to mirror-
I trash the gift
And accept the mirror.

This Is How I Feel: My Life In Verse

Naked

They say that the meaning of
The Naked Dream
All depends on your reaction to your nudity
Compared to everyone else's.
Well,
I still have the Naked Dream.
I'm standing in the middle of the mall
Or walking down the city streets
Just to notice that I am completely naked-
And I'm mortified,
Even though no one else seems to notice.
In the latest version of the dream,
I try to cover up with a towel,
But you know the average towel
Can hardly cover a normal sized adult,
So…?
So I'm walking the halls
Crowded by people who couldn't care less
About my awkward attempts to cover my flesh,
But I fear more than death
The moment someone says,
"Look at the naked girl."
I carry that fear into real life every day.
I fight with my Mississippi Mass of locks,
Line my lips and eyes,
Accentuate some curves
While adequately concealing others,
Spray myself with something sweet,
And adorn myself with jewelry that shines and clangs,
All in an effort to keep people from saying,
"Look at the naked girl."
At some point in the day,
That fear subsides.
I join in the laughter of my colleagues
And feel like I'm blending in
When I smile into that next face-

Dimonique S. Boyd

Not knowing until it's too late
That they will snatch away my towel and say,
"Look at the fat girl."

UnConscious

I'd rather dress to cartoons
Than the local news
Because today's missing child
Is next week's dead one.
I drive through this city
Plagued with potholes,
Liquor stores,
Crack whores,
And street corner memorials.
I give impromptu tutorials
To young men who can't keep their pants up
And young women who can't keep their skirts down,
Who frown upon using financial aid refunds
For books and supplies,
But seem so surprised
When they find themselves on the other side
Of the University doors.
I work with Christians who say
"Bless you"
Like it's interchangeable with
"Fuck you"
And play mental checkers with women
Older than my mother
When they're REALLY supposed to be teaching me
Chess.
I rest my head in hands
That red-ink essays
Written by children who write
As if English weren't their first language,
Wondering if I should blame the parents
Or DPS…
I spend at least 20 minutes a week explaining
Why I do NOT-SUPPORT-KWAME
And facing crucifixion
Because I refuse to accept Oprah as my God.
I watch minstrel shows on BET

Dimonique S. Boyd

Put on by people
Who don't know the meaning
Of 1865
Or understand the history of that blood
That keeps them alive
I
See Willie Lynch Theory
Killing my community
And feel powerless to stop it
I see the powers that be profit
From our ignorance
Or indifference
Or flat out greed
And still people feel the need
To call me out on the carpet
For "being on that love shit?"
I'm anything BUT unconscious,
In fact,
I'm up half the night
Pondering the plight of my people,
But even revolutionaries make time
To make love,
And excuse me
If one day out of the week,
I choose to speak love,
Or lust,
Or something other than this war that will forever rage
And though we're on the same page,
What revolutionaries tend to forget
Is that there is no revolution
Without love.
The revolution wasn't started just because shit wasn't right
The protests aren't just for progress,
But for love of the people who the changes will progress.
When stress rains down
It's love that rubs their backs

And gently nudges them back into the fight
And late at night
When the fists come down
The hands extend
The limbs expand
Get tangled,
And
Tiny Revolutionaries take root…
I can't live with my fist up.
There are some things that you just need two hands for.
I need two hands to raise my nephew
To teach him to count to ten,
To clap for his successes
To console him when he fails.
I need two hands to counsel these youth
One to snatch the brothas britches up
And the other to point in their chests.
I need two hands to clasp together
And pray for the state of this world
And ask God what my ministry needs to be…
Well, I did ask
And He
Said my revolution is Love…
And if that's still not conscious enough for you,
Then excuse me while I slip back
Into my coma.

Dimonique S. Boyd

Word Wrath

People think me timid
Because I don't run toward confrontation.
If anything,
I respect words too much
To use them in vain
So I refrain
From letting my mouth
Win the race with my brain.
And maybe I take on too much pain,
Because I know that hurt climbs into bed with Anger,
And Anger is a lover
Easily roused
And hard to rest
So I try my best
To feel the Lord's arm around my shoulder
And His hand over my mouth
Until I am able to assess the situation…
BUT-
Once it has been assessed
And been upgraded from a situation
To a problem,
I can feel my tongue pulsing,
Truth at the tip of my tastebuds
Threatening to explode
I can taste these verbs
Trying to squeeze the essence out of my nouns
Made more pronounced by adjectives
Describing my objectives
And I fully intend
To spend the bank of my frustrations
On your verbal castration-
I know a lot of words and I know how to use them.
See,
I can throw fifty-dollar words at you
And you'll probably be too confused
To be offended

Or I can come at you on the common
And make sure you feel the full effect
Of my literary wrath.
The difference between
Knowing a lot of words
And knowing how to turn a phrase
Is the difference between
Having a big dick
And knowing how to fuck
And in that respect,
I'm a damn good lay…
I'd rather pass wisdom than wrath
But in the aftermath
Of persistent ignorance,
Sometimes a spanking works better than a speech
And should I reach the point
Where I have to teach my point
In a manner not quite suitable of a lady and a scholar,
I am almost certain
That you will never again
Question my silence.

Dimonique S. Boyd

Explanation/Freeing Myself

I don't get to be what I feel
In real life
So I live
I love
In my pieces
I live
In two-sided college-rule
Or single-spaced 8 pt font
I want,
Need,
Lust in these lines
But you can't just trust in these lines
Because there is so much more of me
To know.
I blow
All my provocations
Into this mic
Like a lover's ear
But there's no lover here
So if it appears
That I spit a bit too intimately
That's just me
Daydreaming out loud
In front of a crowd.
These thoughts crowd my mind
And pulse through my body
And the only way to make them cease
Is to release them into the atmosphere
Until my palate is clear.
Sometimes I fear that you think me vulgar.
Sometimes
My sensuality overcomes me
And one piece can't contain the whole experience
So what starts as one poem
Becomes a series
And sometimes

This Is How I Feel: My Life In Verse

The lucky man doesn't even know
He's the fodder for my flow
Sometimes I forget myself
And I'm too honest
Sometimes I forgive myself
And I'm too honest
Sometimes I accept myself
And I'm just honest
Because honestly
I live
I lust
I love
I want
I need
To be freed…
So I free myself
And I hope
That you won't judge me
For feeling
Just a little too free.

Dimonique S. Boyd

Beautiful

I wanna feel beautiful.
I wanna grin
When the sun's rays kiss my skin
I wanna be more than comfortable in the skin I'm in
I wanna feel beautiful.
I want the sheer audacity
To hear pretty girl songs
And think they're talking about me
I wanna stay out of modeling
To give other girls a chance
I wanna dance with the sparkle
In my own eyes
I wanna cover all the mirrors
So I won't get mesmerized
I wanna feel beautiful.
I wanna feel as beautiful
As the most beautiful woman I've ever hated on
I wanna
Look at men dead on
And make them feel shy
I wanna take your breath and not even try
One day before I die,
I wanna feel beautiful.
I wanna feel as beautiful
As new life
As true love,
Hope,
Dreams,
As God's very promises to me.
I wanna wrap my heart around myself
And love harder and deeper than I loved any brother who tried to break it.
I wanna get soul naked
And feel
Beautiful.

CHAPTER FIVE

This is how I feel about Sensuality/Sexuality

Dimonique S. Boyd

I tend not to like erotic poetry because some poets don't know how to draw the line between erotic and pornographic-or they do and they simply CHOOSE pornographic prose. I am a more sensual person by nature, be it in my writing, the music I listen to, or even what I choose to eat. I feel that all of my pieces are sensual in that they are layered and textured. I try to engage as many of the senses as possible to convey the best interpretation of my feelings. However, I chose to make this the Sensuality/Sexuality chapter because I don't consider these pieces Erotica. Although these pieces allude to things of a sexual nature, I find that I write from a more sensual standpoint- at least for the most part... ;0).

Sin

I was sinning.
I was sinning so good.
I was sinning til my soul felt the singe,
But I was sinning in love.
I was sinning like tomorrow wouldn't come
And there was no Heaven anyway.
I sinning like there was no sin in it…
Shit,
It didn't feel like sin.
I was loving and touching you
Feeling like I had my arms around
The part of myself
God left to be found.
I found you
And we made the sounds
That sinners in love do
I
Sinned with my hands
My lips
My tongue
With all my skin and hair
I didn't quite let you go there
But still,
I sinned.
Then I took a rest and did it again.

Dimonique S. Boyd

Selfish

It's not like me to be selfish
But right now
I want to monopolize all your time
Knock down every cobweb
And explore the recesses of your mind
Taste your every thought
Cloak myself in your emotions
Then be the recipient
Of all your motions
I yearn for your every move
To result in
Your skin
Touching mine
When you blink
I want to feel your lashes
Brush my cheek,
Want your every breath to warm
Then cool
My flesh
And I really don't care
If you think I'm being fresh
Just
Fuel my love
And feed my lust
Give me your heart
And all of your trust
Then
Fill me to the rim
With all your thrusts…
Whisper your secrets
Into my hair
As I feel your heartbeat
Against my back
And when we fall asleep in each other's arms,
Dream of me.

WordPlay

It ain't easy for me to admit this,
But fuck it-
I'm like Sunday Morning for you…
Or maybe you're just that good.
See,
With words alone
You achieve as much
As a lover's touch.
A lot of brothas boast about their word count
But haven't learned how to make their words count…
With one word you do me in
And one word isn't enough
So do me again…
Please?
When you
Tap the keys
It's like you're
Tapping me…
Lyrically speaking.
Your keystrokes turn to kneestrokes,
Kneestrokes to thighstrokes to…
You know what comes next.
You effortlessly convert text to sex, you
Strip me with your words
They fondle me under my clothes
Making me flush…blush beet red
Some nights I can't wait to go to bed
And think about the things you said
And while I can't get you out of my head
I'd be remiss not to mention that
I give impeccable word myself.
My words tiptoe right up the hairs on the back of your neck
And rest on your earlobes
Nibbling their way into your consciousness
Making subtle suggestions

Dimonique S. Boyd

Bold claims
And clear utterances
But if you still can't hear me,
I'll speak directly into your mic
Softly and intently
Gently caressing each letter to the letter
You won't want for a phrase,
I won't waste a syllable,
And trust me…
I have a nickel slick tongue
And a platinum vocabulary.
I spit verbs
That make you chant adjectives
And incoherent expletives
Til you're depleted.
And when our wordplay is completed,
I'd never drop your mic
And walk off stage…
I'd ink it with my signature
And kiss it goodnight…

Goodnight.

WordPlay 2

I can't wrap my arms around you at night
So I grip this Bic
And write
Until my hand cramps
And I date-stamp
My latest homage to what you make me feel inside…
But I think I've done enough writing for now.
I want to see what flows from the tip of your pen
I'll gladly be your inkwell
You can
Come inside and write all over my walls
You can
Draw masterpieces
Or
Tag them with your graffiti
Express yourself neatly
Or spill ink all over my floors
The space is yours
To fill
With your quill
I submit to your will
And I won't stifle your creativity
I have a proclivity
For your brand of art
You're a genius in portrait and landscape
Your brilliance overflows the page
And I've got good stationary,
But you soak every sheet,
Unwilling to leave any piece
Illegible
Or incomplete-
You can cover me in tattoos
That make grooves
That specifically fit you
You can custom me
In any design you choose

Dimonique S. Boyd

I blush
When I think of you approaching me
With your brush
I spread my canvas wide
In anticipation of your latest work
Anxiously awaiting
Becoming
The manifestation
Of your interpretation
Of me.

Secret

I tend to be open.
REAL open.
I don't mind sharing
What others tend to hide
And sometimes
I let other people inside
When I shouldn't
And I'd take some back if I could…
But listen.
Me and you?
Let's make a secret.
Let's make a secret so delicious
That I just want to hold it
On the tip of my tongue
And savor it,
Praying that it doesn't trickle
From the corners of my mouth-
You dare me to spill.
Dare me to tell the world
Of our night of thrills
And I'll practice my restraint-
It'll be like verbal S&M.
Tempt me to tell
But I'll only tell it back to you
Hotter than it occurred
Spurring the beginning of yet another secret.
Two little secrets
Sizzling on my tongue
Hot like lava
And I still won't
No matter how you
Prod,
Poke,
Or provoke
No matter how you stoke my flame
I won't tell a living soul

Dimonique S. Boyd

Of our after dark antics.
Satisfy me to secrecy.
Love me so thoroughly
That you steal my words
Then whisper them back to me.
Make me wanna reveal my words
Then touch me in places that make me remember
To conceal my words
Lest I not get a third secret to keep…
Yes,
Let's make a secret.

This Is How I Feel: My Life In Verse

Pheromoans

Something about you
Grips me like a vice
Every time we share air
Your energy pulls at my center
Heightens my awareness
Of my womanliness
The sound of your voice
Tiptoes up my spine
And lingers on the nape of my neck
We've barely said hello
And I'm thinking about sex...
But don't look at me like that
Because I know you remember
When I touched your cheek
And it made you groan
But we don't need to speak
We communicate through our pheromones-
Or rather
"Pheromoans"
I sense your scent
And I want to get you alone
I was already with it
When I saw your number on the caller ID
Now that you're near me
I want you next to me
Undressing me
You're hexing me with your eyes
I can't wait
To hold your weight between my thighs
To leave my evidence
If they dust you for prints
I want all roads to lead to me
DNA swabs
Will return my heritage
Plus my brand of toothpaste
What I see and smell

Dimonique S. Boyd

Makes me want to make haste
To touch and taste
To hear our pheromoans
Sing in muffled tones-
But first I need to shut this front door...

Wanting...

I wanna get closer
Than skin to skin
I wanna breathe you in
By the molecule
I wanna know you from head to toe
Every mole
Every pore
Translate every slight of your breath
I wanna
Know the source of your pain
By the taste of your teardrops
Show up at your door
Just as you're thinking of me
I wanna know
Who
What
And how you be
What it takes to set you free
Cause I want you to feel free
To make your home in me.

CHAPTER SIX

This is how I feel about Male/Female Relationships

Dimonique S. Boyd

I am a relationship poet. I have many hobbies and interests, but I am most interested in human nature, and particularly in male/female relationships. Again, I never went through that stage where boys were gross. If boys had cooties, I wanted them...LOL. But seriously, out of all the things a person could want from Life, all I want is someone to share my life with. I think about it all the time, which is why this collection of poetry is so heavy on the issues between men and women. I don't mean to be exclusive, but I do write from the point of view of a heterosexual woman.

In my quest for love, I have had many mishaps and met all types. The joke is that I am Carrie Blackshaw, and I write the "Sexless in the City Chronicles." The poems in this chapter-as well as many in previous chapters-speak to those experiences in particular. These are some of my feelings and frustrations with male/female relationships...courtesy of the Carrie Blackshaw Sexless in the City Chronicles.

This Is How I Feel: My Life In Verse

I Can

I can make you come.
I can have you on the freeway
In twenty words or less
I can put stress on your zipper
Make it earn its keep
I can
Wake the beast
And put it right back to sleep-
Don't sleep…
I can make you cum.
I got hydraulics
That make you go hypnotic
My figure eights are legendary
Ain't nothing about me secondary
I can make you cum.
I've got an active imagination
And I'll give you a demonstration
With no hesitation
My every kiss is libation
To get you high with infatuation
I can make you cum.
I can take your body
Where your heart won't go
I can invert your eyes
Make you tell lies
In the throes
I can
Take your mind
Off the rest of these hos
One lick at a time
I can make you say its mine
I can make you call me "Dollar"
Cause I'm worth ten dimes
I can get you spent
With fore-, during, and after-play
See, I can make you cum,

Dimonique S. Boyd

But I can't make you stay
And the staying
Is the part I actually need.
I need a man who can last
Past coitus
Who
Doesn't ask for sex
Before he asks for my name
Never realizing
That he's focusing on
The wrong point of entry.
I need a man
Who's committed to getting to know me
So that he can properly
Perform foreplay
Mentally and emotionally.
We
Should already be making love
Before we make love.
We should be building Love,
Erecting Love on a foundation
That we aren't afraid to stand on
Until my hand is one
You aren't afraid to put a band on…
But maybe that's too real for you.
Or maybe it's an unreasonable ideal to you
But in either case,
Baby,
I feel for you…
I'm sorry that you'd rather fuck
Cause Love hurts too much
And it pains me to see
That all you see in me
Is an orgasm.
There's a gaping chasm
Between what you want

This Is How I Feel: My Life In Verse

And what I need
And I'm not willing to cross the divide
And should you wake up and decide
You want to cross over to this side
Don't bother.
Don't come.

Dimonique S. Boyd

Hard Girl

I'm really not a hard girl.
I just wake up in a world
Where a man might hurt me today
And I choose to err on the side of caution.
I wake up in a world
Where men use handguns to break-up
And bruises make up
75% of my heart already…
But I saved 25 for you.
I saved 25% of my heart
That hasn't been abused
And I don't want to use it
On the wrong guy
Before I meet you.
When I was a little girl,
They called me Princess
And told me stories about ones who
Kissed frogs that turned into Princes.
Well, I'm a woman now
Tired of kissing boys
Who don't turn into men
And I'm far too old to keep playing pretend.
I'm really not a hard girl.
Ain't nothing hard about me
But the way I love
And I gave my love
Fast and free
Thinking the harder I loved
The faster he would love me
But there was no he
Who ever loved me,
And honestly,
I just don't have another heartbreak in me.
I know you see me frowning and think,
"Ma don't want to be bothered."
I'm just concentrating on how to preserve

This last 25%...
It's not so much that I'm
Protecting it for me
As I'm saving it for you
And I know you deserve my whole heart
But I can only unlock it
One chamber at a time,
And I want to offer you
The healthy part
So you can cover it with your salve
Until it permeates
And medicates
All the infected valves with affection.
Maybe this world
HAS made me a hard girl
But I'll be damned if I'm gon' make this easy
Brothas out here need to learn
That they've got some earning to do
And the lessons won't be at my expense.
And yes,
I may have built a fence around myself
But I can still receive messages
Through the links in the chains.
And if you're willing
To try harder than most
Wait longer than most
Prove yourself to be stronger than most
Then maybe
Just maybe
I'll open the gate for you.
The erection of these walls
Is by no means a rejection of you.
It's a testimony
To the strength,
Courage,
And faith it takes

Dimonique S. Boyd

For me to wait for you.
Every day I wait for you;
I look for you
Behind stop signs and lampposts
In the eyes of delivery men
Bus drivers
And random brothas
Praying that we recognize each other…
Yes,
I just may be a hard girl
But if you look deep enough into my eyes
You'll see
That ultimately,
I'm YOUR girl.

This Is How I Feel: My Life In Verse

CockStar

I practice self-censorship
When what I really want to do
Is be immature about the shit
And I know it don't make me look good
But deep inside
We're all just a little hood,
Right?
I want to prepare for you
A feast of insults and expletives
The main course
Being
A hot steaming platter
Of
Muthafuckah,
Who the FUCK do you think you are?
Talking about how many are on your tip…
But tell me,
Just how limber do you have to be
To ride your OWN dick?
Talking all that shit to bitches
Then wondering why
They rain hate on you
And you cry out in anger
Like they hating on you
But does your new love have any idea
That just last week
You spoke of stroking my kitty?
Thought not.
It's a pity you can't see yourself
For the perpetrator you are
Telling pretty lies
To moisten thighs
Then painting yourself
As some kinda misunderstood rockstar
When you're far from it.
Just a common player

Dimonique S. Boyd

Who bails out on the game
When he's tired of playing-
At least until he's tired of the new chick
Now that I think about it
You're worse than a player
Cause you're a good man
In your own mind
But if you take the time
To roll back the tape
You'll see that
You fostered false hope in these women
Even if you won't admit it
And I really shouldn't give a shit
Cause I peeped your shit
When you shot that shit
But it makes me sick
That you won't COP to that shit.
Nigga, just cop to your SHIT.
Playing schoolboy tricks
With grown ass women
Who just didn't know you well enough
To know better
Well I knew better
So I knew I better
Not be one of the addressees
Of your open letter
Saying
"Ho's get off me; we'll never be together"
I hope you and your flavor of the month
Will be HAPPY together
I never thought that WE
Would be happy together
But my judgement got cloudy
As my panties got wetter…
Silly me,
Right?

This Is How I Feel: My Life In Verse

All that chit chatter
Doesn't matter in the end
And trust me, nigga-
This here is the end.
This is the end of the line for all niggas
No disrespect to brothas, boys, and men
No more niggas on my watch
Not on my dime
Not another muthafuckin' moment of my time
And I KNOW the NAACP
Buried the "N" word,
But they shoulda buried your ass WITH it
When they DID it…
Get it???
You got enough of my time already
So I'ma blow you to the wind
Like confetti
And as you travel on the hotness of my wrath
Just remember-
You'll always be my CockStar…

Dimonique S. Boyd

Eve

I see you clutching your side…
What began as a mild annoyance
Has progressed into a medical emergency
That you're desperately trying to self-treat…
You've been
Poppin' pills
Cause you
Think you're ill
Even the doctors can't tell you anything
But not only can I diagnose you,
I can dose you.
I got the cure for ails you
I'll ease your pain
When Tylenol fails you
I'll be your Codeine
When all is done and said
I'll get you high
And put you to bed
I'll be the salve
That takes away the itch
I'm that prescription
That stops the nervous twitch
I plant the seeds
That grow what you need,
But honestly,
There's nothing even wrong with you.
Okay…
You say you feel an emptiness
That nothing seems to fill…
You thought that BA
Then that MA
Was gonna make everything okay.
Finding no relief that way
You got that good job
Making that good pay
Bought houses and cars

Lived it up like a RockStar
And that still didn't get you far
So now you're sitting there thinking…
Nothing makes it better,
Not drinking
Or smoking,
Or clubbing,
Not those notches you keep carving in your bedpost.
And what scares you the most
Is that you counted your ribs
And it seems that one side has more
Than the other.
You're just feeling the effects of your very first surgery…
You're just missing me.

Dimonique S. Boyd

I Hate Love

I hate Love.
I hate Love
Because it's neither
Late,
Nor tardy,
It is truant.
It is purposefully absent.
It willfully evades me.
But as much of a cynic as it's made me,
I still
Love
Brothas.
I love the way brothas love each other.
I love that 10 brothas
Can be friends
And 10 years later
10 brothas
Are STILL friends.
I love how brothas hug each other
With no pretenses.
I can
Close my eyes
And hear the impact
Of two brothas making contact
Be it dap,
Grip,
Or a pound.
I just love having brothas around
I love the sound
Of their laughter
Feeling the essence
Of a masculine presence
I love the way they smell
From African oils
To designer brands
From the sweat on their brows

To the dirt on their hands
I'm yelling in the stands
Cuz I'm their number one fan
I love brothas.
I love poetry brothas with ink-stained souls
I love blue collar brothas in shoes with worn soles
I love original Hip-Hop brothers who remember De La Soul
Even brothas who actually like Cirque de So-
Leil…
I love brothas who know when to play,
When to lay,
When to stay
And when it's time to gracefully walk away.
I love brothas with a passion
Even at a time
When it seems Love is no longer in fashion
And speaking of Love,
Did I tell you that I hate it?
I hate Love.
I hate Love
Because it's neither
Late,
Nor tardy,
It is truant.
It is purposefully absent.
It willfully evades me.
But as much of a cynic as it's made me,
I still
Love
Brothas.

Dimonique S. Boyd

Thank you for reading "This is How I Feel: My Life in Verse." First and foremost, I'd like to thank God for giving me a productive outlet for my feelings. This book has been many years in the making, and I couldn't have done it without the love and support of my family, my friends, and my poetry home, EchoVerse. I also want to thank every single person who inspired me to write a piece, whether I loved them, they broke my heart, or they simply wrote a piece so good that it made me want to write. I thank Jamar Morris for believing in me so much that he made my book cover for free. I love you, Mar Mar! Special thanks to Brandon Hood for taking the lovely cover photo. You're a modern day Gordon Parks and I LOVE your work!

Last, but certainly not least, I want to thank you, yes, YOU, holding this book in your hands. You have made one of my biggest dreams come true, and I hope you love this book as much as I've loved writing it for you.

Sincerely,
Dimonique

This Is How I Feel: My Life In Verse

www.ingramcontent.com/pod-product-compliance
Lightning Source LLC
Chambersburg PA
CBHW020917090426
42736CB00008B/681